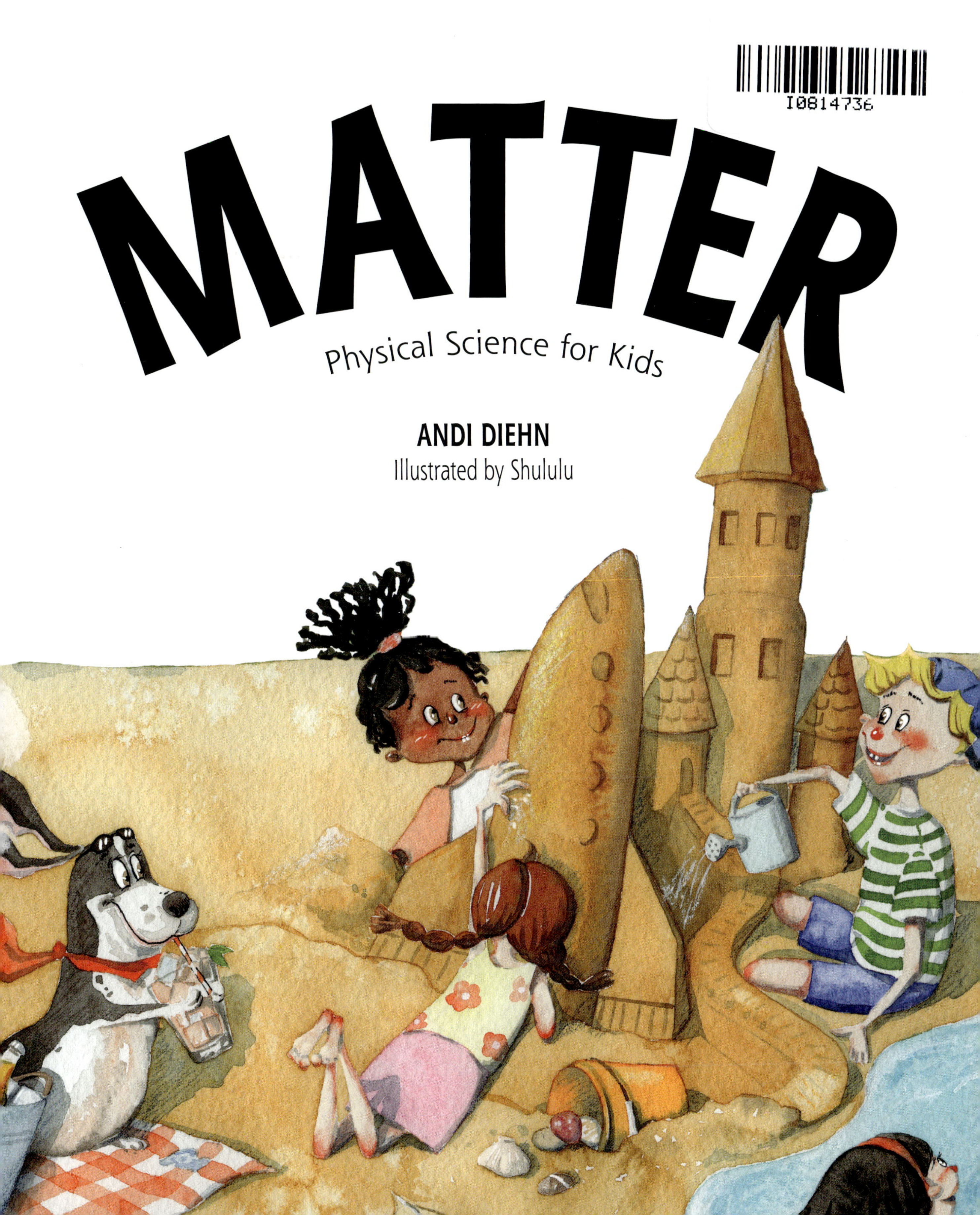
I0814736
MATTER
Physical Science for Kids
ANDI DIEHN
Illustrated by Shululu

Nomad Press
A division of Nomad Communications
10 9 8 7

ISBN Softcover: 978-1-61930-644-8
ISBN Hardcover: 978-1-6193-0-642-4

Educational Consultant, Marla Conn

Questions regarding the ordering of this book should be addressed to
Nomad Press
PO Box 1036
Norwich, VT 05055
www.nomadpress.net

Printed in the United States.

Other titles in this series:

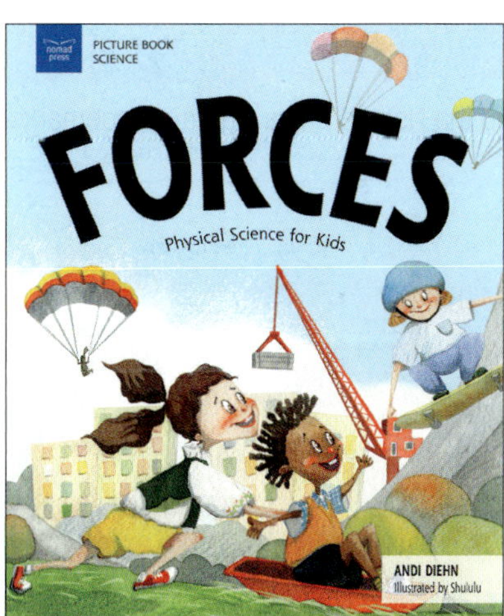

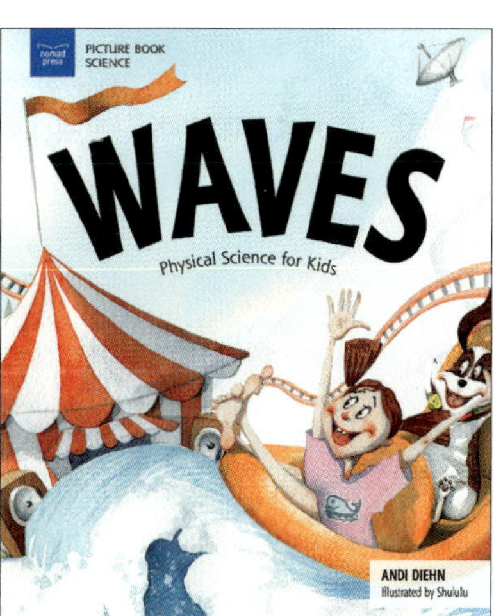

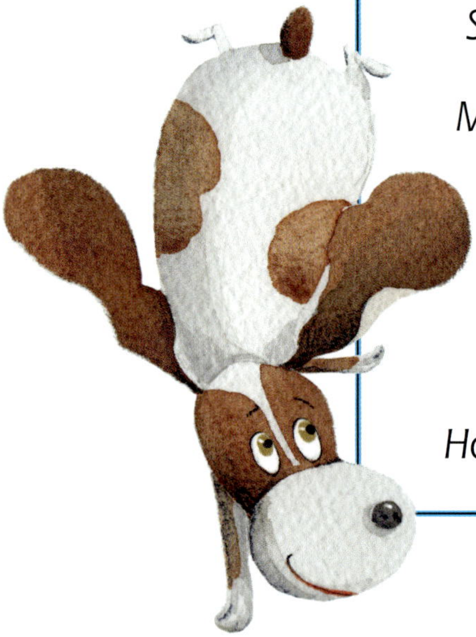

Birds in the sky and rocks
on the ground,

Things made of matter are all around!

Solids and liquids and gases, too,

Make up the world, including you.

Matter is everything,
everywhere you look.

Well, almost everything—

How can you see to read this book?

If your friend looks sad, you might ask,
"What's the matter?"

Matter is something that can be wrong.

When something is the matter, a good friend helps you feel better. Maybe they share a cupcake with you. Maybe they stand on their head and make you laugh.

Maybe they just sit close by
and wait until you feel better.

Have you ever heard someone say, "That doesn't matter!"?

What if you spilled your cup of water? Your teacher might say, "That doesn't matter!"

What if you used your brother's toothbrush?
Your brother might say, "That doesn't matter!"

(But probably not. **Yuck!**)

Matter is more than something that can be wrong or something that happens. **Matter is much more!**

When scientists talk about matter, they are talking about the stuff that makes up almost everything in the world.

Your dog is made of matter.

That tree is made of matter.

You are made of matter.

Matter is anything that takes up space and can be weighed.

How do you weigh things?

With a scale!

How much do you weigh?

How much do your shoes weigh?

How much does your dog weigh?

How much does that tree weigh?

What about air?

Is air made of matter? What happens when you blow air into a balloon?

The balloon stretches bigger and bigger and bigger. The balloon might even pop!

Blow up two balloons so they are about the same size. Tie each balloon to the ends of a ruler. Tie a string to the middle of the ruler and hold the ruler by the string. Move the string so the ruler is completely straight across. Ask an adult to use a pin to poke a hole in one balloon.

» **What happens to the ruler as the balloon loses air?**

» **What does this show you about air?**

TRY THIS!

Because the balloon gets bigger when you blow air into it, you know that the air takes up space.

Air is made of matter!

What about juice,
water, and milk?

Are those things
made of matter?

When you pour juice into a cup, the cup full
of juice is heavier than an empty cup.
You can see that the juice takes up space.
And when you drink the juice,
your belly feels fuller!

Many things are made of matter,
but everything looks different!

You look different from your dog.
Your dog looks different from your milk.
Your milk looks different from the steam that
comes from a pot of boiling water.

Matter can have many
different shapes,
colors, and sizes.

Matter can be a **solid**, **liquid**, or **gas**.

Do you have ice cubes in your freezer? What happens when you leave an ice cube on your kitchen counter?

It melts into a puddle of water! And if you leave that puddle of water on the counter (unless your mom makes you clean it up!), it . . .

DISAPPEARS!

Can you name 15 things that are made of matter—five solids, five liquids, and five gases?

TRY THIS!

Plasma is another state of matter. Have you ever watched a lightning storm from your window? **Lightning is a plasma!**

You know what else is made of plasma? The sun and all of the stars. There's more plasma in the universe than there are solids, liquids, or gases.

What are some things that are not made of matter?

Look around you. Can you see something that doesn't take up space and can't be weighed? How about sound? How about rainbows?

How can you see to
read this book? **Light!**

Does light take up space?
If there's lots of light in a room, does
that mean other stuff has to get
shoved over to make enough space?

Can you hold light in your hands?

Can you put light on a scale and weigh it?

How would you keep it all together so you could weigh it?

Light is not made of matter.

Light does not take up space and it can't be weighed.

Heat is another thing that is not made of matter.

Can you think of more things that aren't made of matter?

Most things are made of matter. Your home, your classroom, and your neighborhood are all filled with matter.

Take a walk—you'll find matter all around you.

The next time someone says,
"It doesn't matter,"
you can tell them,
"Everything is matter!"

GLOSSARY

gas: one of the states of matter. Air is made of gas.

light: something that makes it so we can see.

liquid: one of the states of matter. Milk and juice are liquids.

matter: anything that has weight and takes up space. Almost everything is made of matter!

melt: when a solid changes into a liquid.

plasma: one of the states of matter. The sun, stars, and lightning are made of plasma.

scale: a tool used to measure the weight of something.

scientist: someone who studies science and asks questions about the natural world, seeking answers based on facts.

solid: one of the states of matter. This book is a solid.

weigh: to measure how heavy or light something is. Usually, we use a scale to weigh.